Harn Museum of Art
University of Florida
Gainesville, Florida

This catalogue has been funded
by a special grant from the
AEC Charitable Trust

SPONSORS

**The local sponsor for this exhibition
is The Gainesville Sun, a supporter of
the arts**

**Special appreciation is extended to the
administration of the University of Florida**
John V. Lombardi, President
Elizabeth D. Capaldi, Provost
Gene Hemp, Vice-Provost

**Harn Museum exhibitions and
programs are sponsored in part by:**
The State of Florida, Department of State,
Division of Cultural Affairs and the
Florida Arts Council
Harn Museum Program Endowment Fund
The Harn Alliance
The Museum Store
The University of Florida
Private Donations

A portion of the museum's general operating
funds for this fiscal year has been provided
through a $112,500 grant from the Institute
of Museum Services, a Federal Agency that
strengthens museums to the benefit of the
public.

LENDERS

American Associated Artists, New York
The Bailey Collection, Toronto
Center of the Earth Gallery, Charlotte, North Carolina
Edith Dee Cofrin
Gerald Feffer and Monique Yingling
Gallery NAGA, Boston, Massachusetts
Nohra Haime Gallery, New York
Jeff Joyce
Tobi Kahn
Robert and Nancy Magoon
Curt Marcus Gallery, New York
Marlborough Gallery, Inc., New York
Robert Miller Gallery, New York
Private Collections
Bruce Robbins
Mary Ryan Gallery, New York
Schmidt-Bingham Gallery, New York
Jack Shainman Gallery, New York
Peter Solow
Edward Thorp Gallery, New York
Hiram Williams

ACKNOWLEDGMENTS

The concept of **Destiny Manifest** is both timely and fascinating. It particularly suits our broad campus audience because it addresses many issues that are part of curricula: not only the art historical issue of reviving traditional painting techniques and the question of beauty, but also issues involving conservation, environmental protection, and visualization of the future of our planet. Ethical, moral, and economic concerns are posited along with aesthetic ones.

Budd Harris Bishop
Director
Harn Museum of Art

To produce an ambitious endeavor of this scope is a real test for a university art museum the size of the Harn. It involves the considerable tasks of conducting adequate research, securing sufficient funding, and, especially, obtaining the necessary loans of exceptional art works to fulfill the exhibition's objectives.

We are fortunate to have the personnel talent and to have secured the donor resources to meet these tests, and we owe a deep debt of gratitude to the numerous artists, collectors, patrons, and galleries who responded generously to our requests for loans and information and who guided us to other sources. We extend our enthusiastic thanks to all of our lenders, whose names are listed elsewhere in this publication. We express our profound appreciation to the AEC Trust, a private charitable foundation, for generously awarding full funding for the production of this catalogue. We also offer our warm thanks to The Gainesville Sun for sponsoring the Gainesville showing of the exhibition.

Our Curator of Exhibitions, Dede Young, was responsible for all aspects of this exhibition and deserves particular recognition. She originated the idea; conducted extensive research to refine the focus of the exhibition; visited countless exhibitions, collections, and studios to view work; and negotiated with the lenders for works that she felt were essential to the project. She could not have gained access to all the sources to whom we are now indebted without the active assistance of Dr. Douglas F. Maxwell, Adjunct Assistant Professor of Arts at New York University, consulting curator of contemporary art, and practicing psychoanalyst, whose unique perspective and extensive knowledge were invaluable to the project and who wrote the introduction to this catalogue.

Our entire staff was, as always, engaged in the successful realization of this exciting venture. To Dede Young and her colleagues at the Harn Museum of Art, we extend our sincere thanks for a spectacular exhibition.

Douglas F. Maxwell
Adjunct Assistant Professor of Arts
New York University

If it is fair to say that the predominant attitude of American landscape artists in the nineteenth century was fueled by a search for the sublime as they traveled the Americas in awe of nature and in search of a spiritual experience, then it follows that as the American expansion ended and the world became a seemingly smaller and less remote place, artists were forced to look inward for a similar depth of spirituality.

Could it be a coincidence that at the turn of the century while Freud was making strides in understanding the mind and uncovering the unconscious, the great Modernists of the early twentieth century were utilizing the landscape in the development of abstraction? Then, during and after World War I (further evidence of a shrinking world), Dada and Surrealist artists began to explore the landscape of the dream. In America, artists like Marsden Hartley, Arthur Dove, and Edward Hopper who had looked toward European modernism returned their focus to America and created landscapes that appeared to reject the earlier avant-garde optimism and gave rise to an air of disillusionment.

By mid-twentieth-century, Mark Rothko, Willem De Kooning, Jackson Pollock, and the other Abstract Expressionists were making epic paintings that were simultaneously heroic and disillusioned. As they sought to free the formal stricture of the figure-ground relationship, they utilized their own unconscious processes to create the first landscapes of the mind. Surely the vibrant reds and yellows used by several of these artists in the mid-1950s symbolized an acknowledgment of the apocalyptic potential of an oncoming nuclear age and a continuing Cold War which touched all mankind.

With the exception of Alex Katz and Hiram Williams, all of the artists represented in this exhibition grew up after World War II. Katz and Williams make paintings reflecting a continuing dialogue with Abstract Expressionism. Katz uses color to define psychological mood, and Williams, a witness to the horrors of the second World War, uses the ambiguity of abstraction and perspective to create a metaphor which transforms the landscape into various body parts.

Living and growing up during the second half of the twentieth century has meant facing a continually shrinking world in which the unimaginable and unthinkable have become commonplace. As a group, the artists represented in **Destiny Manifest** have confronted their work by utilizing the precedents of the past to create a freshness in the present which embodies an integration of the universal with the personal. Jacqueline Bishop, for example, travels, as did Edwin Church, to South America, not to be in awe of nature but rather to document its endangered status. Similarly, artists Neil Jenney, Alexis Rockman, Adam Straus, Mark Innerst, and Peter Edlund all emphasize environmental concerns while at the same time alluding to personal metaphors about the human predicament.

Like Katz and the Abstract Expressionists, Bruce Robbins, Irene Valincius, Pat Steir, Peter Solow, and Dozier Bell use color and line to create psychological mood. The device of using ominous or tumultuous landscapes to reflect human emotions arises from the portrait painting tradition in which, as background, the landscape symbolized the complexity of the sitter.

And, like Williams, Tobi Kahn, April Gornik, Jerry Cutler, and Jeff Joyce reference parts of the body in the landscape in order to emphasize our own personal relationships with the elements of this earth. Pressing this to the fantastical are John Alexander, Alan Bray, and Robert Ferrandini.

Although all of the artists are finely aware of and draw upon art historical references, David Bierk, Joan Nelson, Holly Lane, and Wade Hoefer begin their landscapes with a particular historical perspective and contemplate it in accordance with today's world.

Finally, one observation about the group of works as a whole: they are all without people, yet the human presence is profound and signals the depth of spiritual experience contemplated as we look forward to a new century. Despite the aspects of disillusion, the glimmer of hope and optimism shines as a persistent beam throughout **Destiny Manifest**.

Dede Young
Curator of Exhibitions
Harn Museum of Art

It has taken more than three years for **Destiny Manifest: American Landscape Painting in the Nineties** to evolve into this exhibition, which seeks to reintroduce the traditional genre as new and relevant to the contemporary discourse of art. The exhibition includes the works of twenty-four American artists who are invigorating a traditional art form with new meaning and a contemporary perspective that is fresh and stimulating beyond the purely aesthetic. No single point of view is presented but rather a broad searching for truth through an open-ended investigation.

Many of the artists in **Destiny Manifest** focus on the changes in the environment as a context in which to reflect the complexities of our contemporary society, creating paintings that push the boundaries between observation and participation. Some are as connected to the body or the mind as to the land, creating landscapes as metaphors of the internal self, of reflection and introspection, revealing dreams of spiritual and psychological transformation. Others present moody or magical landscapes veiled in layers of ambiguous meaning, while still others create narrative or pointedly ironic landscapes. None of the artists feature human figures or man-made structures in their landscapes, but in each painting the presence of humanity is implied. All of the artists are seriously engaged in the process of discovering ways to communicate their sense of the world on the brink of a new century.

Viewed as a collective whole, the artists in this exhibition express the landscape through what might, at first glance, be considered a standard of visual beauty. But, in fact, they have broken free from conventional expectations of beauty to forge a new aesthetic—a testament to the times as demanded by the nature of contemporary human experience. With time, these paintings transpose our initial perception of beauty into an awareness that inherent in these images exist timely subjects for contemplation.

In the nineteenth century a small number of male artists established the American School of landscape painting, which by 1839 was known widely in Europe.[1] Artists such as Thomas Cole, Albert Bierstadt, Frederic Edwin Church, Asher B. Durand, and Martin Johnson Heade struggled with science, religion, and art as they explored and recorded the vast wilderness of the north and south American continents. They, and others like them, aspired to trek into the wilderness to observe firsthand and to portray true images of the natural world with the clear purpose of emphasizing mankind's union with Nature. They carefully copied botanical specimens and cloud formations; they reconfigured observed vistas, synthesizing various details into aesthetically pleasing compositions; they froze dramatic moments such as storms or sunsets in time—all in an attempt to characterize Divine power. Nature was viewed with Romantic passion, recorded as a noble symbol of high morality, a spiritual and physical refuge for mankind. The nineteenth-century landscape painters were entrusted to reinforce the idea of wilderness as part of the national pride and purpose.

When the American School of landscape painting was established, America's prevailing doctrine was "Manifest Destiny," a rationale for expansionism "to overspread the continent allotted by Providence for the free development of our yearly multiplying millions."[3] As recorders of the visual history of America, landscape painters were elevated to a role of extraordinary importance. To the national agenda of their era, nineteenth-century landscape painters demonstrated a continuing loyalty.

In the twentieth century, Americans became disenchanted with the Romantic spirit. The passion for expansionism turned against itself and became inverted as the modern world developed in a mutually destructive relationship with nature. For many, progress was an uncomfortably fast experience, a disillusioning process of simultaneous expansion and contraction. With advances in technology shrinking the world, enabling a plethora of disturbing truths about permanent changes in its condition to rise steadily to the surface, prevailing attitudes grew to regard "Manifest Destiny" and all it implies obsolete. Consequently, as civilization grew, so did individual, national, and international interest in and anxiety about our shared destiny.

New information and experience provide the force which can break new ground for creativity. Artists in **Destiny Manifest** observe the changing world from their various vantage points along the frontier, across generations and gender, and respond through art that symbolizes a new spirit and definition of the landscape.

Neil Jenney's painting *Atmosphere* (1985) is the single work in **Destiny Manifest** from the eighties; it was consciously selected for inclusion here as a work (widely considered at the time) to signify new possibilities for the course of American landscape painting.

Jenney seduces the eye with a beguilingly simple, smooth field of contemplative space that we recognize as sky; no cloud, moon, horizon line, or reflecting pool of water is depicted to organize the view. He works in the manner of nineteenth-century Luminists, such as John Frederick Kensett and Heade, painting a clear image in gradual tonal changes to resemble radiant light.

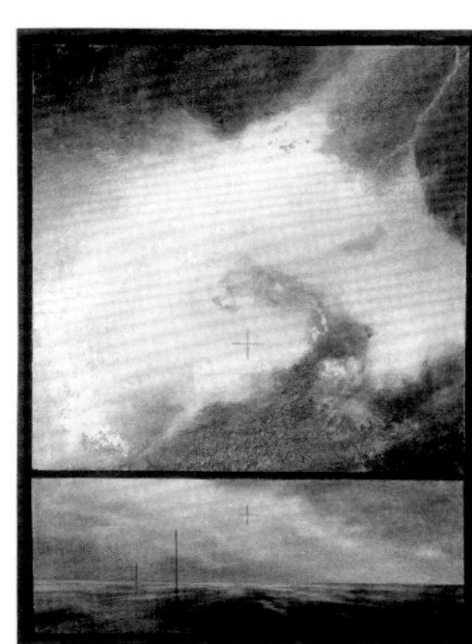

Dozier Bell, *Map #6*

The visibly empty image takes on meaning with the word "Atmosphere" stenciled on the thick wooden frame. The vast cloudless sky, once the symbol of endless bliss, is transformed to a container of the air we breathe, growing more toxic over time as the ozone layer thins. Our initial desire to become visually engaged in this painting of idyllic beauty is disturbed as realities of contemporary existence emerge, and illusion becomes disillusion.

Like Jenney, April Gornik breaks through history, pulling from it a Luminist formalism and infusing it with a feminist perspective. Gornik's glorious landscape *Lightning at Twilight* (1993) is organized into a horizontal expanse of sky, mountains, and water, suggesting a space of "limitless amplitude."[4] She reaches into the realm of the sublime to give this stunning wild place she has envisioned an intensely emotional expression. Lightning flashes and splits the night, characterizing a raging figure with upraised arms to symbolize the female voice, silenced for so long by history, demanding now to be seen and heard.

A quiet mood pervades Jeff Joyce's diptych *Veil* (1993), which reflects Asian painting in composition, tonality, and subject. Mountaintops, rendered with the detail of an Albrecht Dürer, penetrate the atmospheric veil like icons of time and history to suggest an underlying unity or connection with the past.

Joyce's brush strokes create a shimmering overall effect that seems to echo the controlled breathing used in certain spiritual practices to achieve an inner state of quietude. Subtle ambiguities in the space arise from a viewpoint that is slightly above and at a distance, creating a metaphor for physical and psychological disorientation and alienation.

Dozier Bell also plays with mood and dislocation in *Map #6* (1995), a diptych that merges two views in an incongruous juxtaposition. The close-up, meteorological cloud effect of the upper part of the painting is reminiscent of nineteenth-century cloud studies by artists such as John Constable, Jasper Cropsey, and J. M. W. Turner. Alfred Steiglitz's later formal photographic studies of clouds (1923-1932) also come to mind. The long view of the beach on the lower panel shifts to completely distance us, creating a dichotomy of near and far. Bell imposes a series of vertical and horizontal marks on the illusionistic spaces; some appear as cross hairs, like sighting marks in a rifle scope or camera lens, others as faint grid lines suggesting mapping points for human navigation.

Adam Straus' starry nocturne *McStop* (1993) also indicates human presence in a large-scale composition that is predominantly sky. He composes a space that is wide open to summon a sense of awe and grandeur in a view that is, again, from above and at a distance; but here the vista seems to include us. From our high vantage point we see faraway mountains in silhouette, lit from beyond the horizon by a glow of lights. Straus' perspective takes on a note of irony suggesting that even in the remotest places humanity is measurable by the number of golden arches present per acre, inferring that we are becoming McWorld.

Mark Innerst also composes a dramatic open space that is primarily sky, but Innerst's intimately-scaled landscape *Plume* (1994) is reminiscent of a Dutch painting. He bathes the image with a silvery light, achieved by the use of aluminum leaf and acrylic, giving it the tone of an old hand-tinted photograph. He surrounds the image with a wide frame, hand-built in a nineteenth-century style, that contains it, making it precious—like a captured memory.

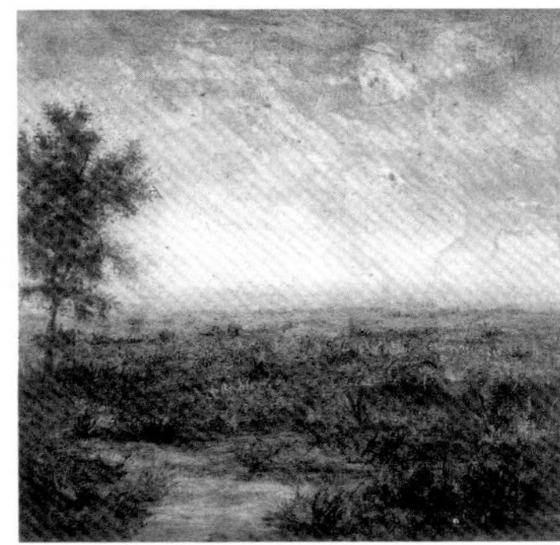
Joan Nelson, *Untitled (#396)*

Low on the distant horizon a white smoke cloud billows, forming a rising trail through the sky, interrupting the vista with an ominous mood indicating destructive forces of humanity.

Like Innerst, Joan Nelson's intimately-scaled painting *Untitled (#396)* (1994) evokes the past, but she excavates it like a Romantic archeologist to create a new fiction from fragments of landscape images she finds pictured in books. Nelson reworks the appropriated details into a classically ordered landscape reminiscent of Albrecht Altdorfer or Jakob Ruysdael. She layers acrylic, oil, powdered pigment, and varnish onto a smooth wood panel, producing a luminous surface with the aged appearance of an Old Master painting, which emphasizes our distance from Nature, past and present.

Also working in the realm of history and appropriation are David Bierk and Wade Hoefer. David Bierk relies on reproductions for his images, but he prefers to appropriate entire paintings which he copies on a reduced scale. In *A Eulogy to Earth (History), Ancient River* (1995) he pays homage to one of Bierstadt's depictions of the American West, painting the work on steel to symbolize modern industrial society. He bathes the image in a golden light, creating an Old Master patina and a luscious surface which he then alters by stenciling the word "history" across the sky, defying the canon he reveres, transforming meaning to convey loss and longing.

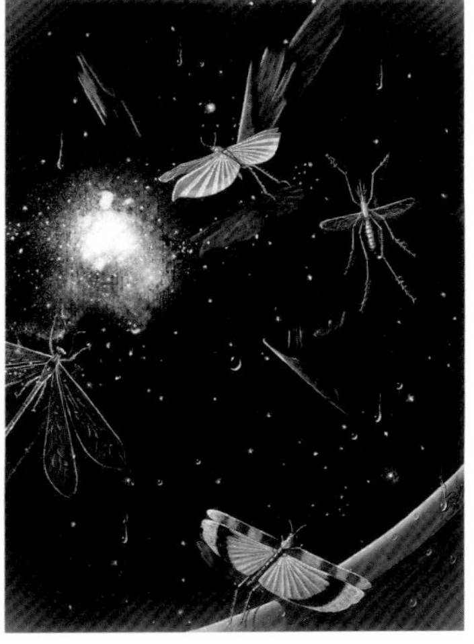

Alexis Rockman, *Biosphere VI*

In *Agris II* (1995), Wade Hoefer creates a dual image that imposes the artistic convention of Claude Lorraine in a classically ordered landscape reflecting humanity's mastery over nature. He paints the composition in the center of a piece of linen that has been commercially printed to look like a tonal etching depicting a kind of historical anthology composed of classical ruins, sailing ships, and hunters – subjects reminiscent of artists such as Nicolas Poussin and Claude. The pre-printed cloth creates a border around the pastoral scene, giving a double meaning to the frame of history on the progress of culture.

The nineteenth-century theme of artist as natural historian is perpetuated in the work of Alexis Rockman, Jacqueline Bishop, and Peter Edlund. For Alexis Rockman the remaining frontier is the future. In *Biosphere VI* (1992) beautifully rendered flying insects exist in a glass structure that appears to float in space, back-lit by a starry night sky. The view seems to be from the inside out, one in which we are contained with these species, but are at the same time seeing them close-up, as though through the lens of a microscope.

Rockman's environmental view becomes disorientingly free-floating, signaling extreme disruption in the earth's ecosystem and indicating a fearful destiny, where the future is chaos and freedom is lost, where the earth becomes ultimately uninhabitable, and survival is limited to a small, contained environment somewhere in the solar system.

Jacqueline Bishop's landscape *System of Nature* (1990) also contains beautifully rendered species, but hers are the flora and fauna of the Amazon. Like Heade and Church, Bishop gathers data firsthand, traveling to South America to observe and record abundant and disappearing species. Placing her data bit by bit in a pyramidal composition that becomes a unity in itself, she creates a jungle landscape framed by bare trees and a blazing hot sky that reflects the persistence, interconnectedness, and fragility of the natural world while signaling a disturbance in the biodiversity essential to survival.

Bishop partitions the canvas like an icon painting into three connecting panels, giving the work a religious overtone, a sign of her hope. A human fetus the size of a tropical flower floats at the top of the pyramid, connected to the life force of the jungle below by an umbilical that grows from a plant stem, a powerful symbol of future generations and the symbiotic relationship between humanity and nature.

Peter Edlund also creates a landscape in which everything is to be understood in terms of interconnection. In *Archives of the Earth* (1996) he paints a lush bed of flora and fauna with an Old Master quality. The form of a fallen tree in a state of decay becomes strangely familiar. The process of metamorphosis here recalls paintings by Giuseppe Archimboldo, alluding to notions of life, death, and transformation both organic and bizarre.

Working between abstraction and representation, in *November Night* (1994-1995) Pat Steir flings paint which dissipates on a dark ground in a pattern that seems to measure the cosmos and the random order of the stars. Looking up, away from the traditional horizon, she reaches into the void of the night sky for contemplation. With an additive approach to painting tied to artists such as Jackson Pollock and Morris Louis, Steir comes very close to a realistic portrayal of distant stars, giving us the position of observers to question where we are.

Bruce Robbins' abstract *Horizon* (1996) appears to be a composition of simple forms that echo the shapes of treed mountaintops. He builds up a surface that is both dense and luminous, setting up an open space with contrasting elements of thick and thin, dark and light, top and bottom. Then, seeking to integrate the internal with the external, he carves a continuous line through the layers of paint and encaustic, marking his conscious and subconscious impulses, as he expands the plane into an infinite space vibrating with energy, alluding to the once endless wilderness that existed in harmony.

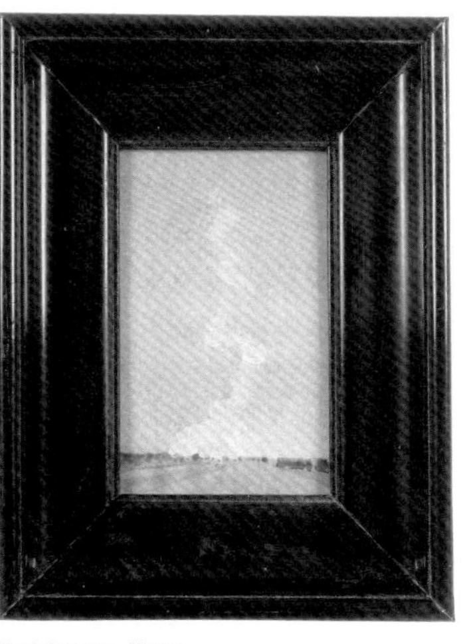

Mark Innerst, *Plume*

In *Mystical Events Over Bald Eagle* (1992), Hiram Williams also employs abstract simplicity to suggest a denuded mountaintop pressing at the boundaries of the space. Williams' image reflects a dialogue with modernism and existential philosophy. In polar opposition to nineteenth-century ideals of finding spiritual union with nature, Williams' landscape becomes a metaphor for the struggle of internal and external worlds in a seemingly unresolvable predicament. Verging on nihilism, the landscape appears as a scarred skin, replete with the irony of the spiritual crisis of humanity confronting its mortality.

Working in the realm of biomorphic abstraction is Tobi Kahn, whose forms show ties to artists such as Arthur Dove and Marsden Hartley. Kahn builds up layers of paint to model a raised, textured surface that is saturated with color. In *NAAHM-HWA* (1994), organic shapes that at first appear to be an aerial view of the sand and sea shift to internal, microscopic forms that can be read as cell-like. The title reflects the word of a rhythmic chant, which, through repetition, can eliminate superfluous information in the process of drawing outward energy inward, toward a complete state of balance and harmony.

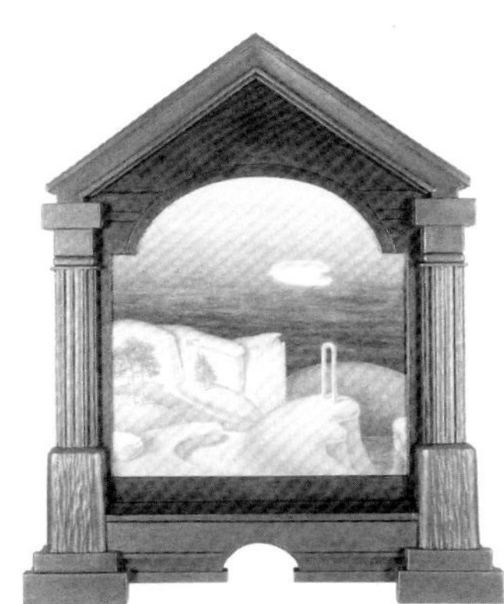

Holly Lane, *Before Nightfall*

The deep emotional impact of color in Peter Solow's nocturnal seascape *Off Montauk* (1996) is balanced by the gentle rhythm of light on water that reinforces its overall effect of constant movement. Solow paints his subject from firsthand observation, creating an image about sensation. He is concerned not only with the surface appearance of the water but with the intervals between its peaks. His self-revising brushstrokes accumulate in a search for illusive certainty in a world whose state is one of constant change.

In *Fugitive Series: XIII* (1994), Irene Valincius spreads her canvas with wax and interference powders in translucent layers that seem to float and remain liquid, creating a surface that appears to glow from within. She achieves a reflection of a moment of light-bathed beauty that embodies an emotional, enigmatic quality that transcends traditional light effects. As in Solow's work, the image seems to continually move. Valincius' central light spreads colors, from warm to cool, that appear to change in intensity as the viewer moves by.

John Alexander paints rocks—a subject that recalls Gustave Courbet and Paul Cezanne—in *Bridal Path* (1993), a composition verging on the surreal. His lively brush work gives vitality to a landscape that exists in the moment after some force has shaken it, evoking a sense of instability and memory of unseen wild and/or human dramas.

Jerry Cutler's central form in *Monument* (1993) is a deteriorated tree that stands like an ancient figure; a sentinel to the passing of time. Cutler paints in a style reminiscent of Regionalist artists such as Grant Wood and Alexander Hogue. He recalls his childhood on a rural Wisconsin farm and creates forms from memory that suggest an internal landscape with a network of leafless trees running like nerve paths through plowed fields that undulate like rippling muscles. The disputable fertility of the soil hints at the psychological struggle created by searching the past to reconcile the present.

Like Cutler, Alan Bray in *Fresh Snow* (1996) reinvents and orders a Maine landscape that is also reminiscent of Regionalism. Flatly painted with hard edges and details all equal in importance, his fallen trees, bleached like old bones, capture the character of a landscape that has changed very little over time. Like Winslow Homer, Bray finds his subject in his own backyard, depicting a memory that stands for Nature in its own cycle of life and death.

Robert Ferrandini takes the idea of the scenic and skews the view, containing it as a reflection in a view from above in *Gathering Samples Along Crystal Cove* (1994). Ferrandini's watery surface looks soft and aged like a fresco, with vague, time-worn fragments from long ago blended into a single image that suggests artifice and dislocation.

Holly Lane invents a personal landscape inspired by Northern Renaissance artists such as Mattias Grunewald and Jan van Eyck. She hand-builds the elaborate frame around the canvas of *Before Nightfall* (1994), treating it as one piece, like an altar, to present a mythical landscape of great expanse on an intimate scale. Lane's nocturnal landscape is full of mysterious landforms that lead to strange, fantastical dwellings along the edge of a cliff. Across a winding path a narrow, arched portal stands to symbolize passing through time.

In *Wildflowers III* (1992), Alex Katz elevates the ground below, amplifying it to a horizonless panorama of open space and pure sensation. His deft, gestural brush strokes, which relate to abstract expressionism, form grasses and wildflowers that sweep across a green field as if disbursed by the wind, creating an environment we cannot enter.

Katz's field at first appears to be an artificial place without human history, yet it summons the viewer, stirring memories of a personal space perhaps last experienced in childhood.

From the intimately-scaled to the monumental and heroic, the richness and diversity of the works in **Destiny Manifest** demonstrate the passion of these artists for exploring new possibilities for the tradition of landscape painting. Concerned with history and beauty, with the connection between the self and the external world, these artists have created paintings that are both of the moment and enduring. They have succeeded in freeing themselves from the past to bring forward a new vision which symbolizes a new spirit in the American School of landscape. They have significantly pushed the boundaries of contemporary painting with the purpose of characterizing our age, not as prophets predicting what is going to happen but rather as participants revealing what is happening. They also have disclosed an interest in the social function of their work by transforming the history of the genre to reflect contemporary attitudes toward nature. Finally, inherent in **Destiny Manifest: American Landscape Painting in the Nineties** is the notion that our shared history is inseparable from our shared destiny, and the works of these twenty-four artists show us that new frontiers are always there, that anything is possible.

1   Louise Minks, *The Hudson River School*, 1989, p. 12 (New York: Crescent Books, 1989).

2   Barbara Novak, *Nature and Culture: American Landscape and Painting 1825-1875*, 1980, pp. 16-17 (New York: Oxford University Press, 1980).

3   John O'Sullivan, 1845, *US Magazine and Democratic Review*, reprinted in *Larouse's Dictionary of North American History*, 1994, p. 175 (New York: Larouse Kingfisher Chambers, Inc., 1994).

4   Novak, *Nature and Culture*, p. 29.

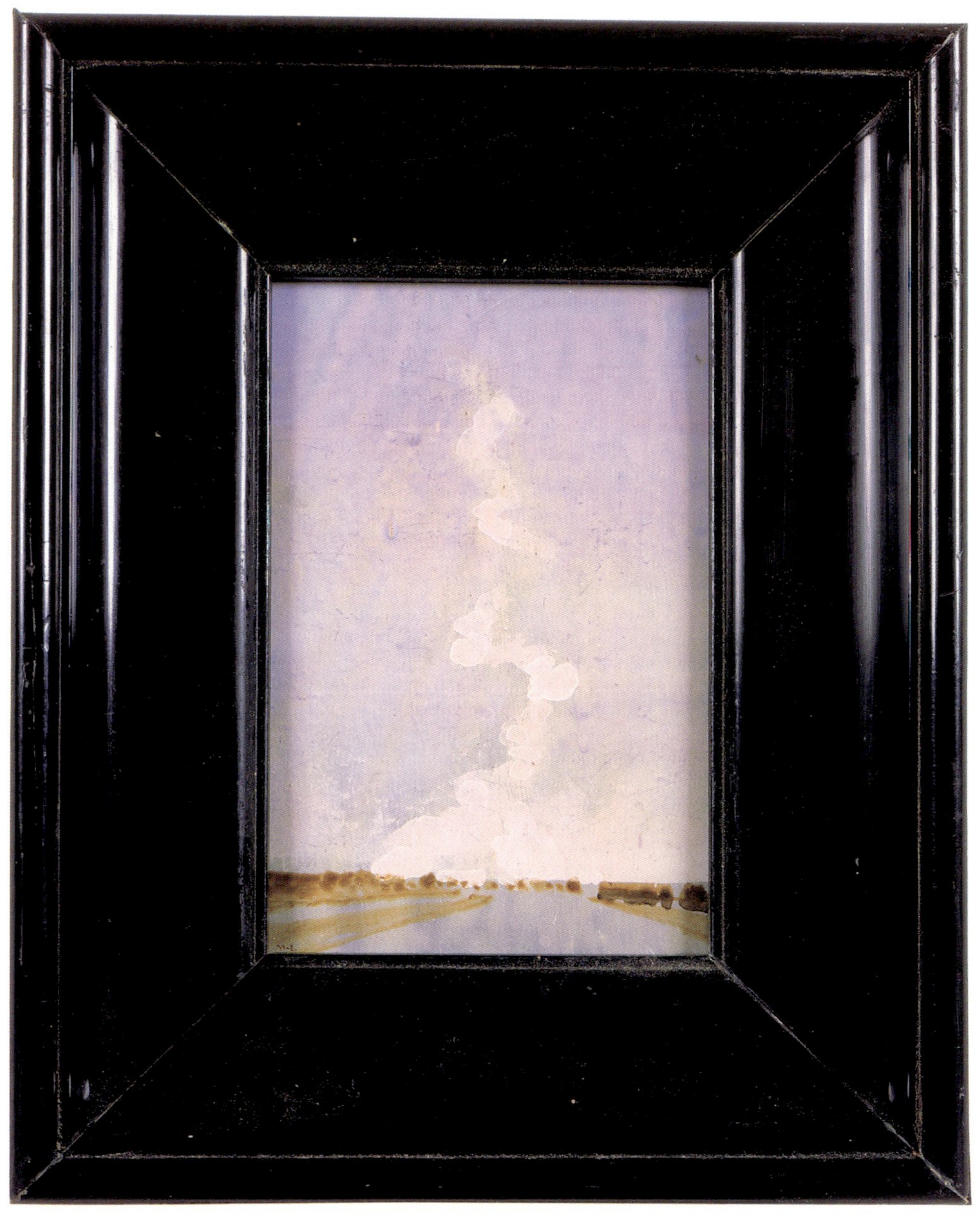

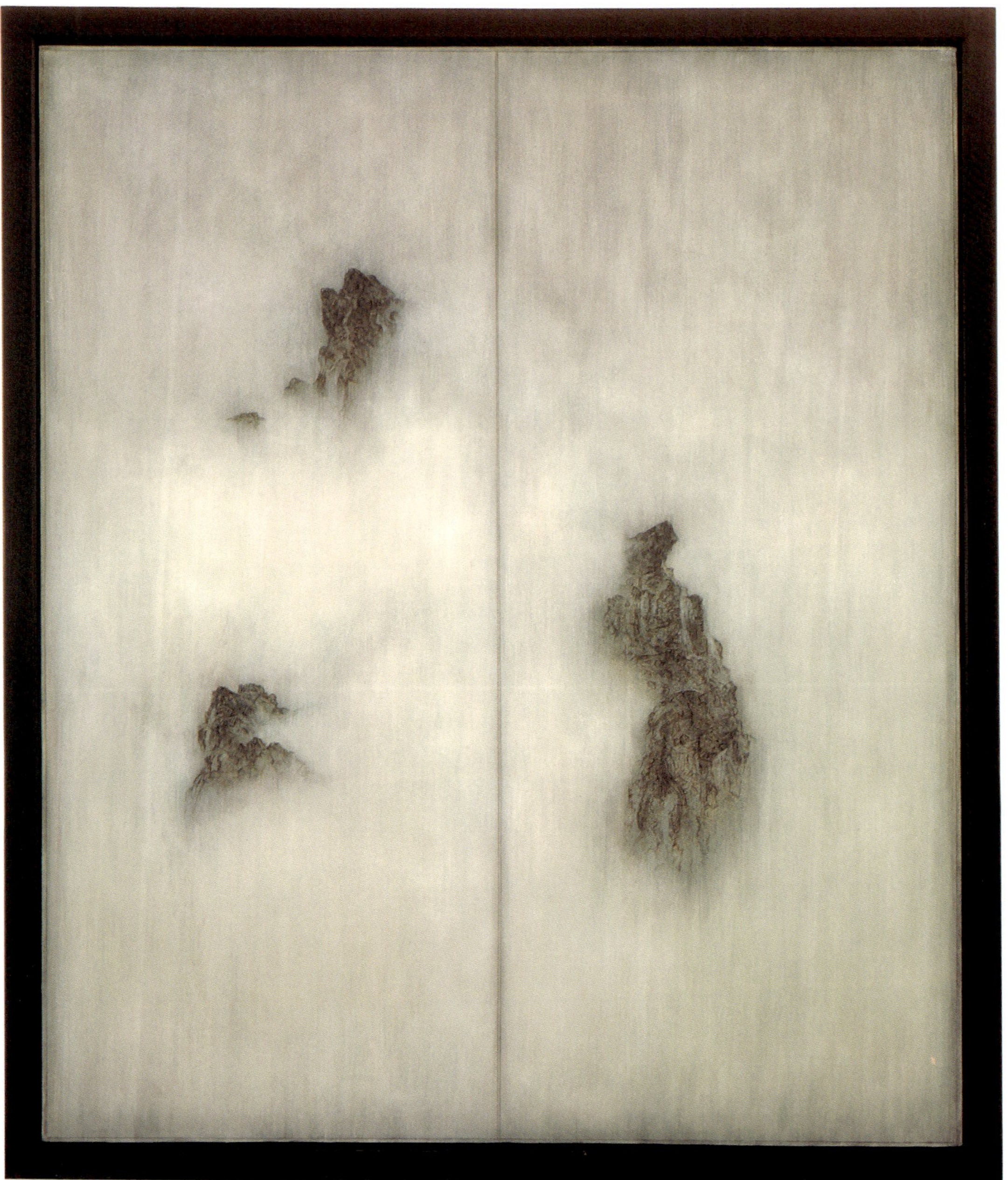

Jeff Joyce
American, b. 1956
Veil
1993
72 in. x 60 in.

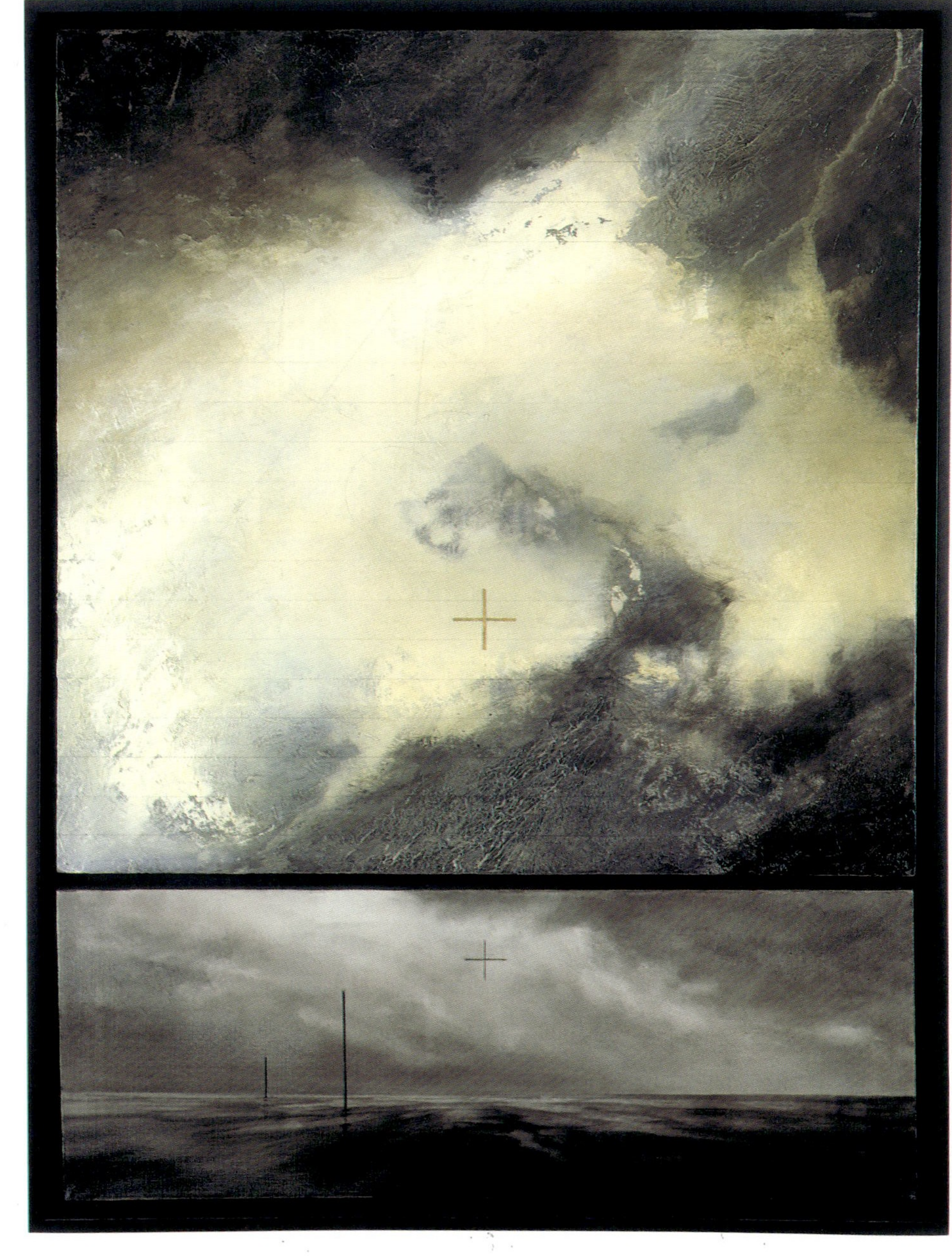

[14]

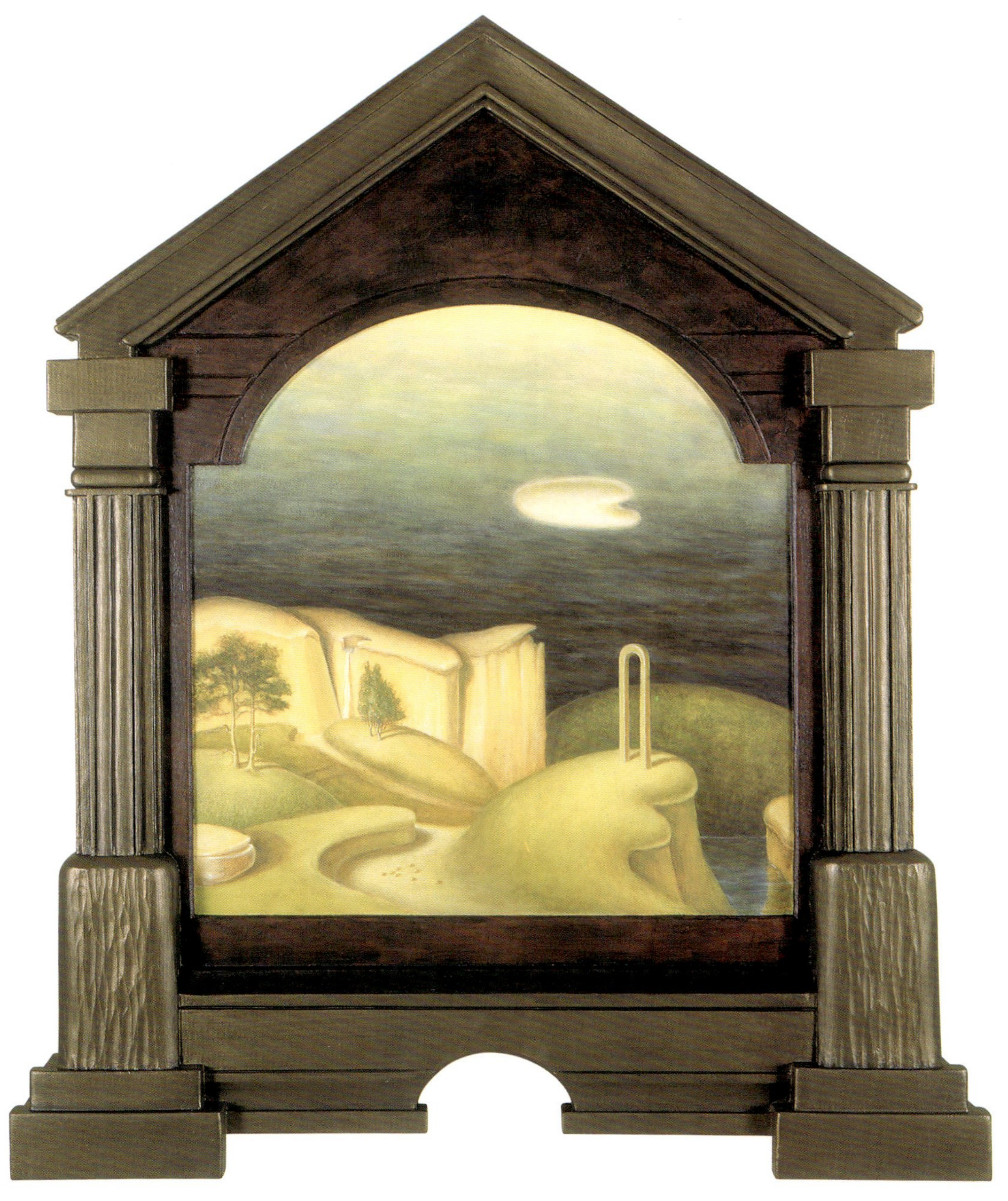

Holly Lane
American, b. 1954
Before Nightfall
1994
29 in. x 24 in. x 5 in.

Alan Bray
American, b. 1946
Fresh Snow
1996
20 in. x 30 in.

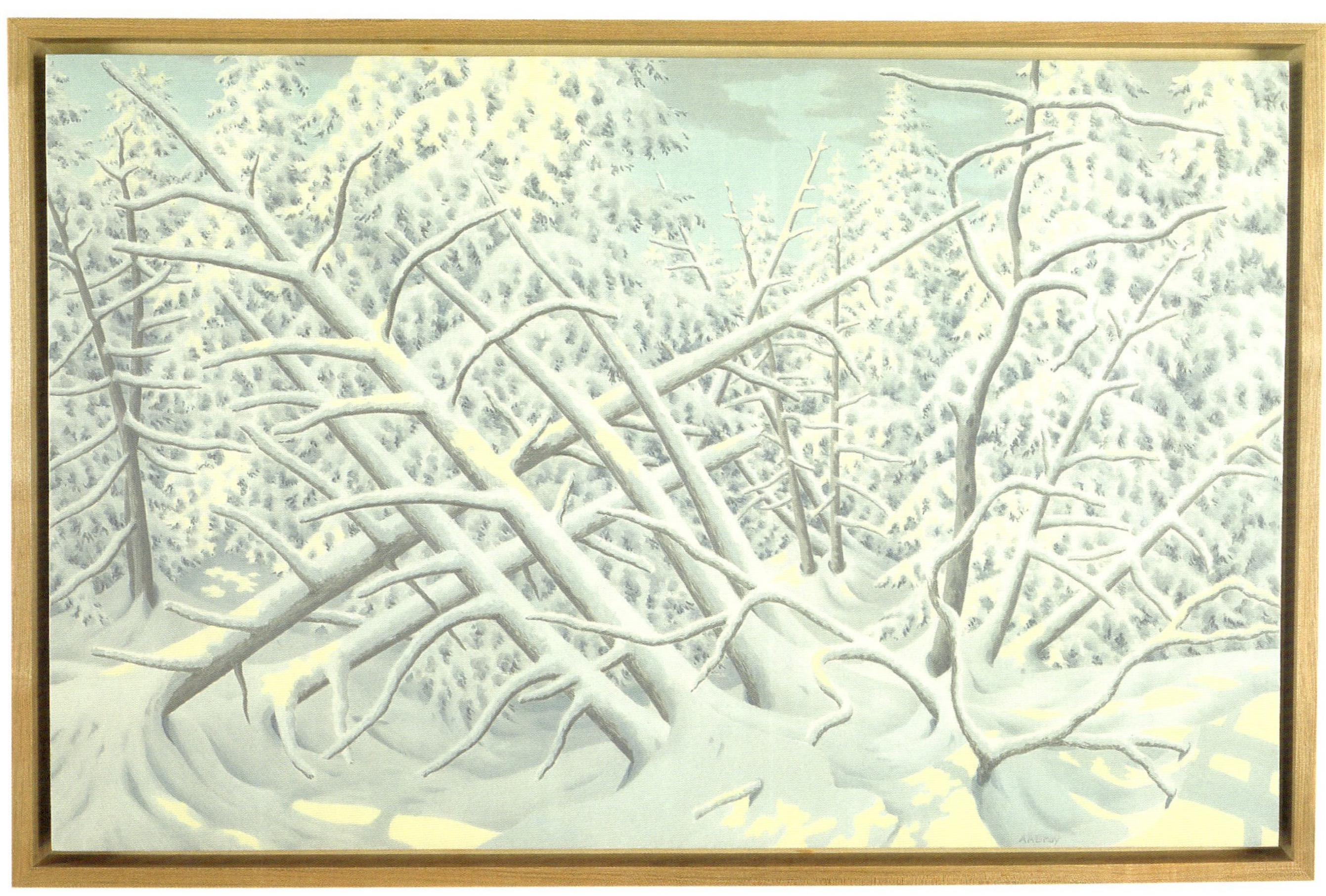

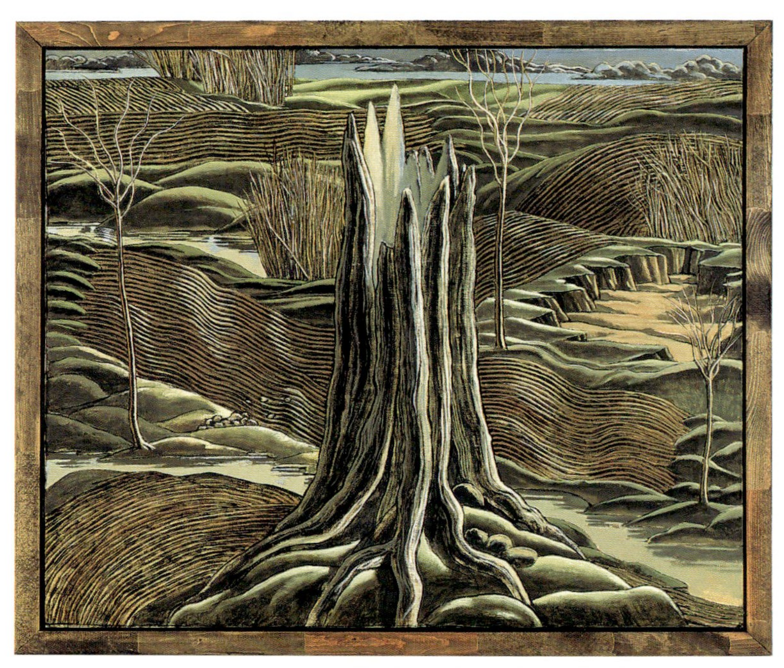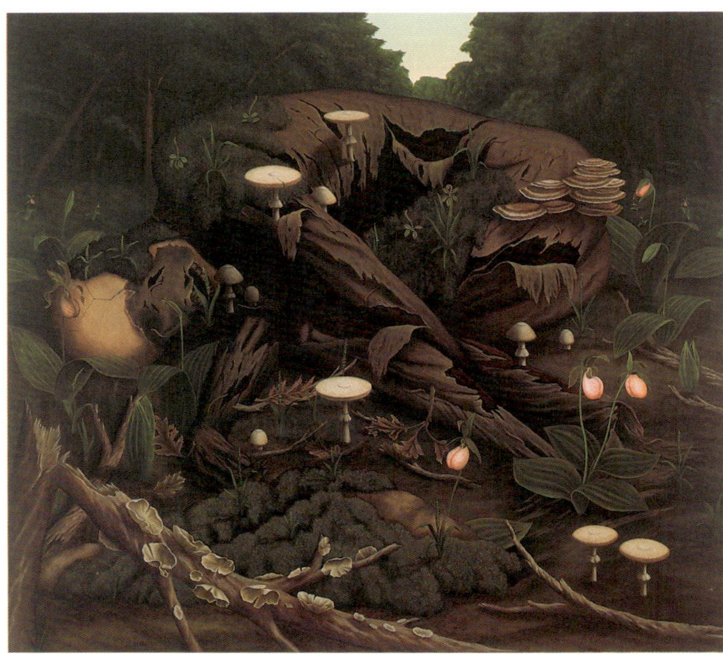

Left:

Jerry Cutler
American, b. 1946
Monument
1993
50 in. x 59 in.

Right:

Peter Edlund
American, b. 1959
Archives of the Earth
1996
44 in. x 48 in.

Jacqueline Bishop
American, b. 1955
System of Nature
1990
18 7/8 in. x 47 5/8 in.

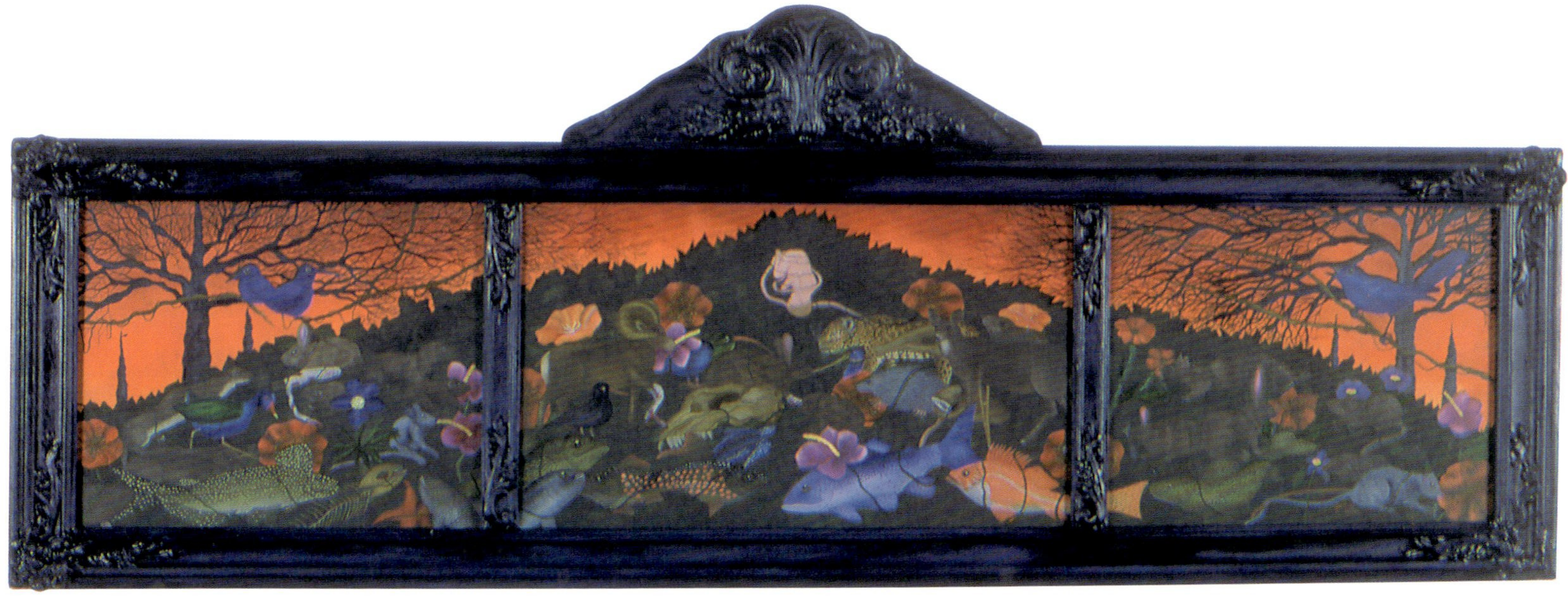

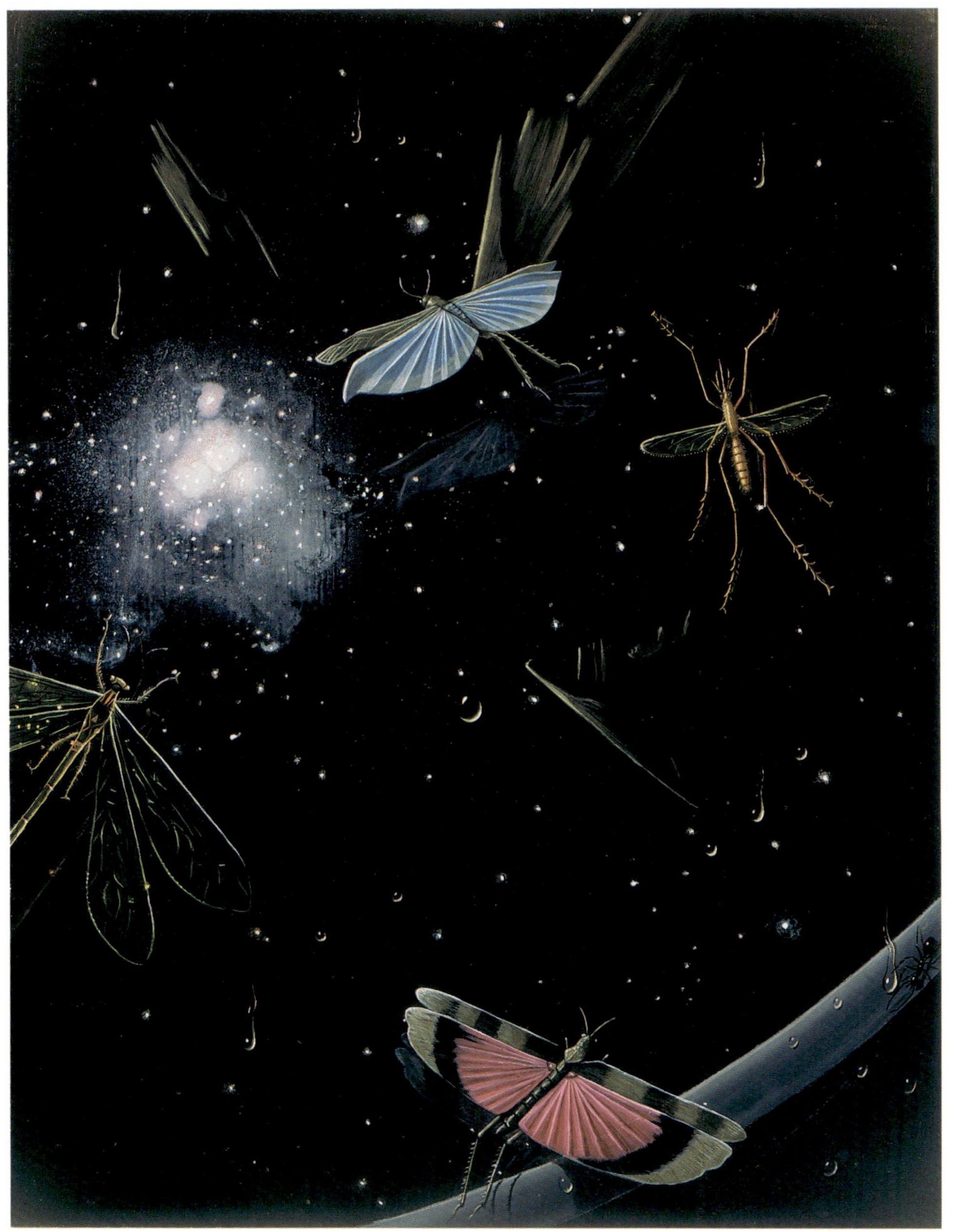

Alexis Rockman
American, b. 1962
Biosphere VI
1992
24 in. x 18 in.

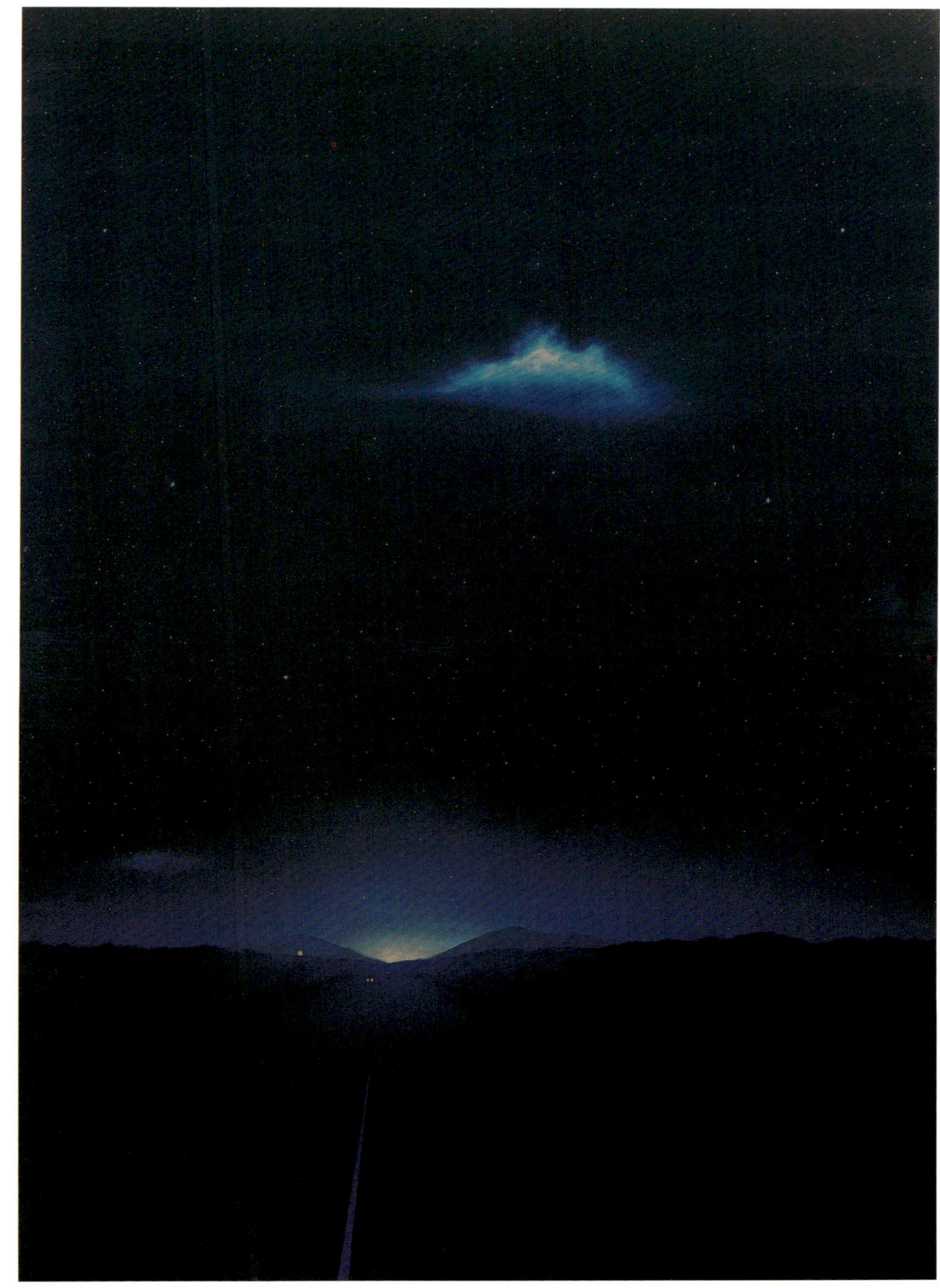

Adam Straus
American, b. 1956
McStop
1993
84 in. x 60 in. x 2 in.

[24]

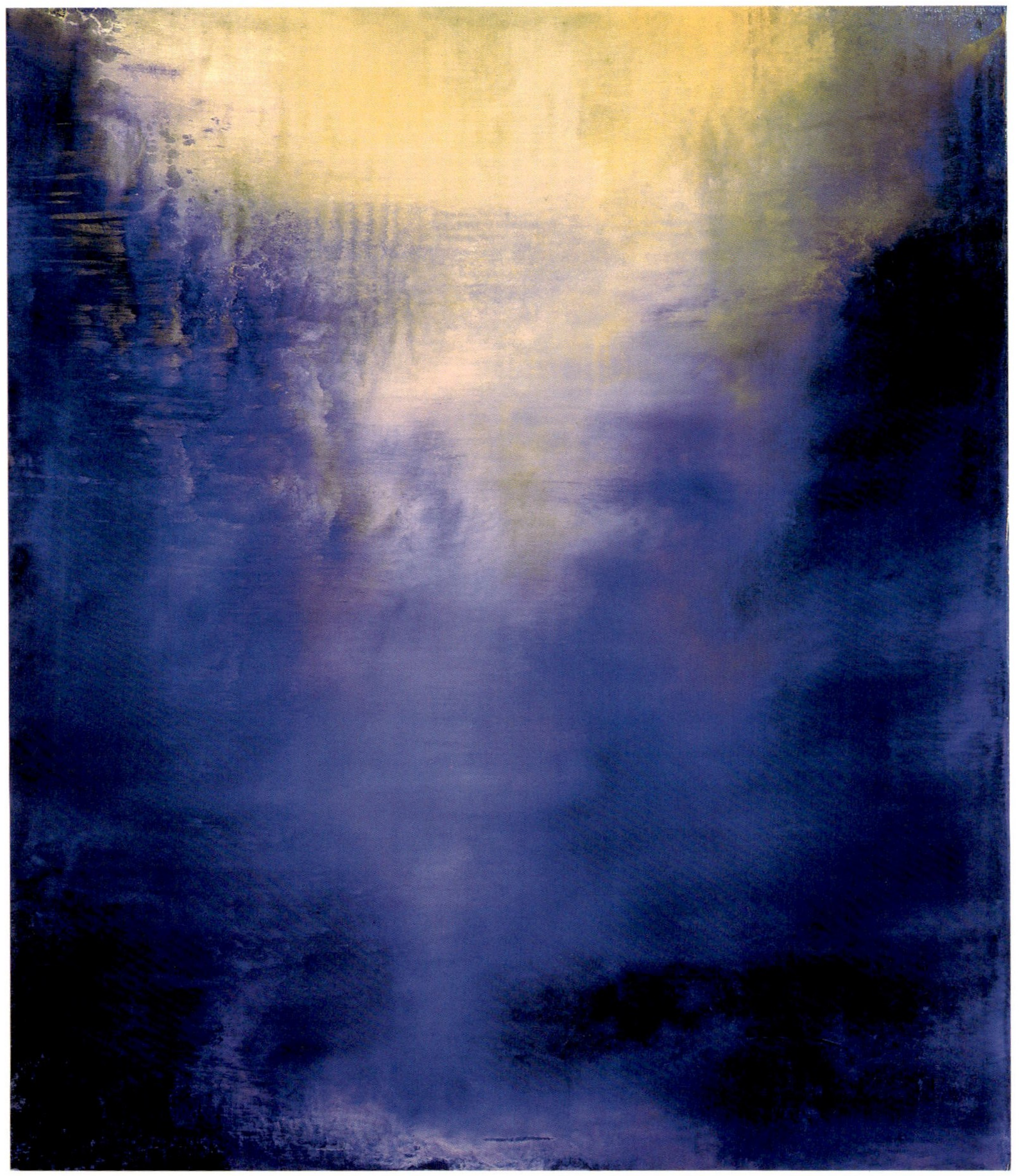

Irene Valincius
American, born West Germany 1948
Fugitive Series: XIII
1994
36 in. x 30 in.

Hiram Williams
American, b. 1917
Mystical Events Over Bald Eagle
1992
50 in. x 86 in.

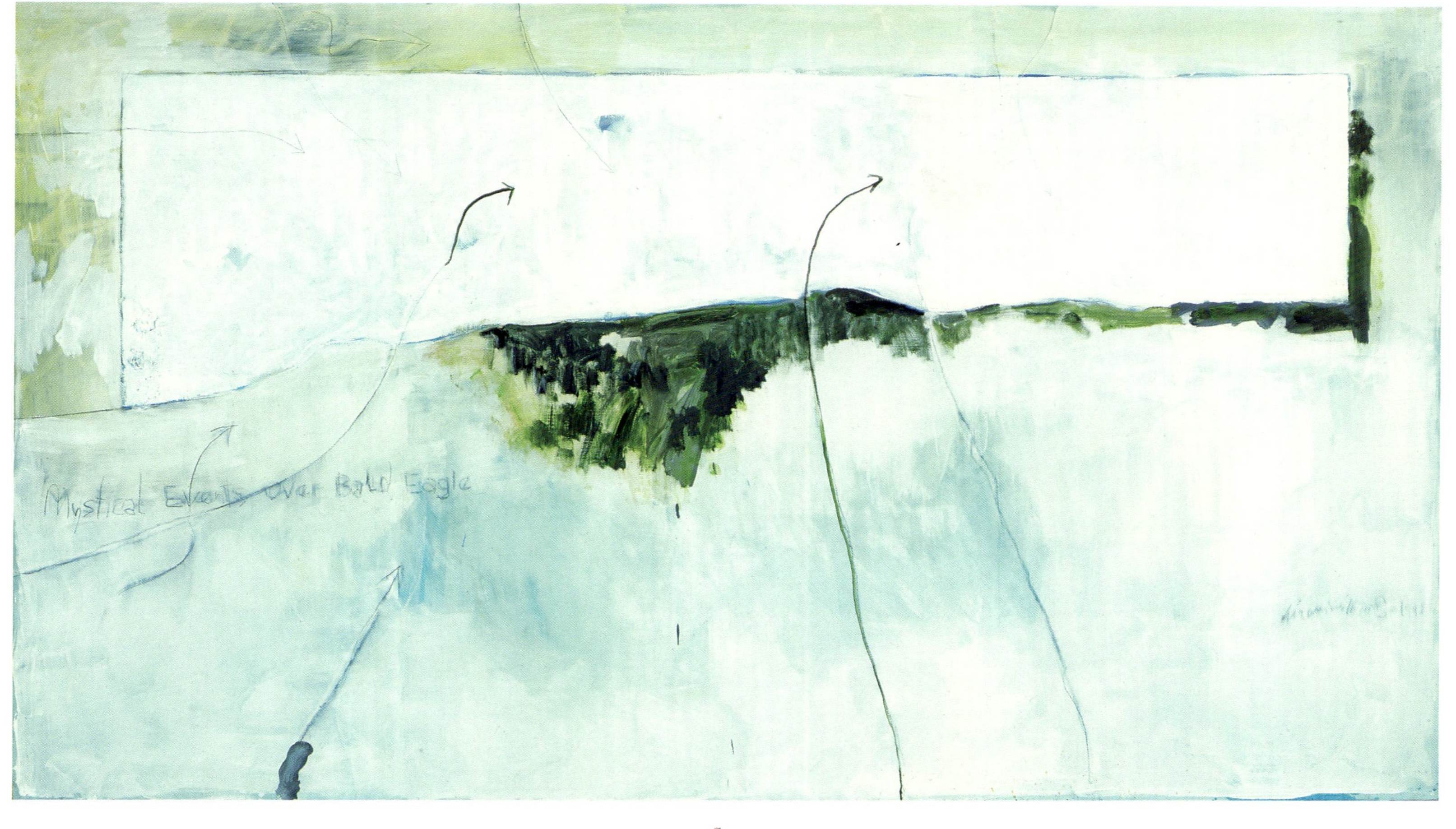

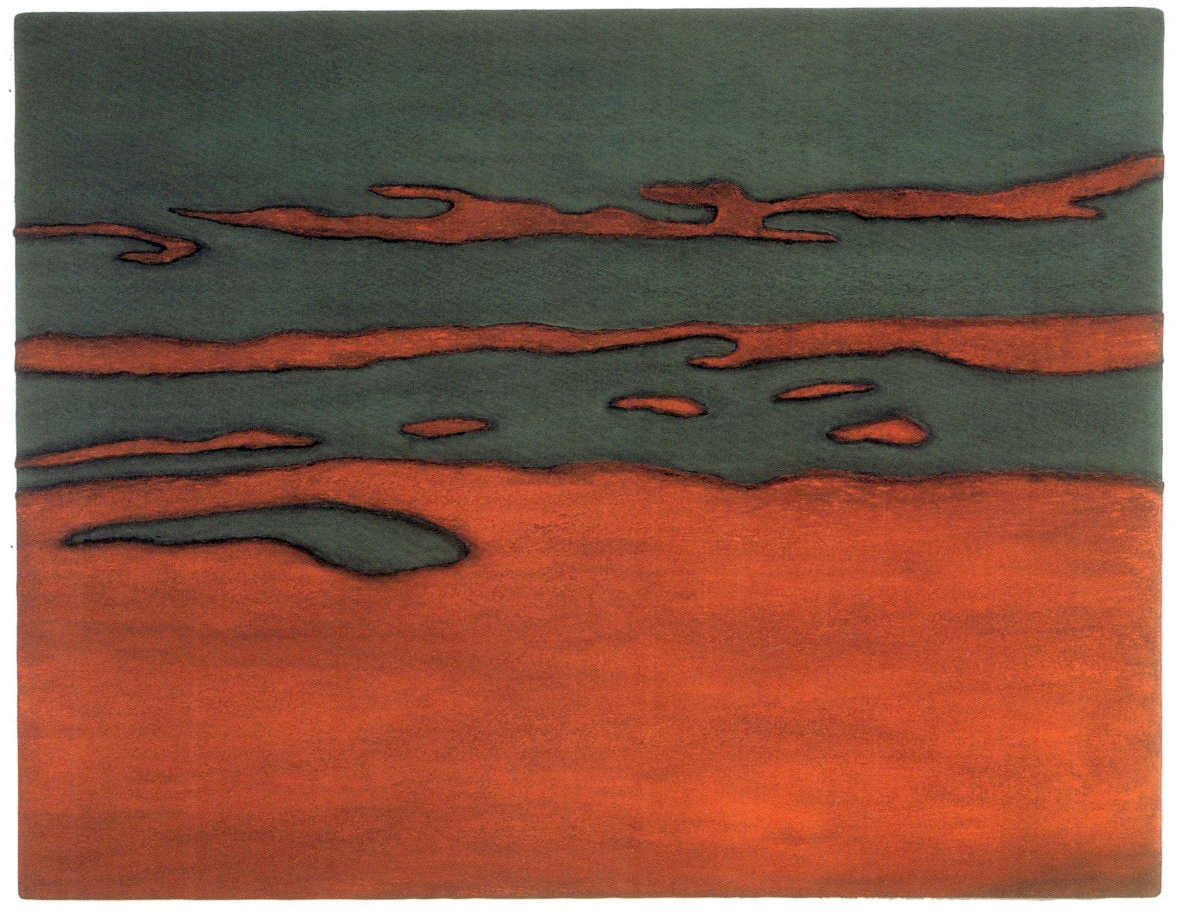

Tobi Kahn
American, b. 1952
NAAHM-HWA
1994
40 in. x 50 in. x 2 1/2 in.

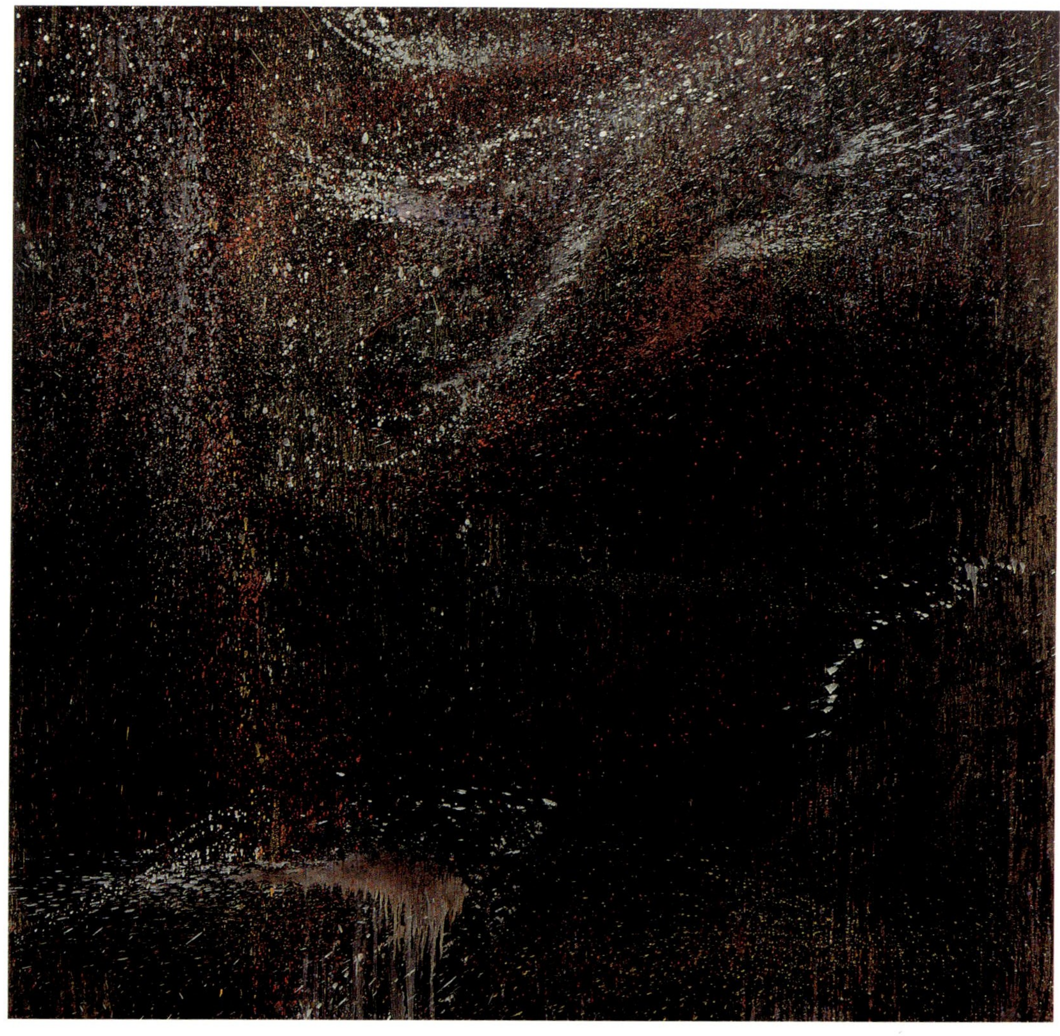

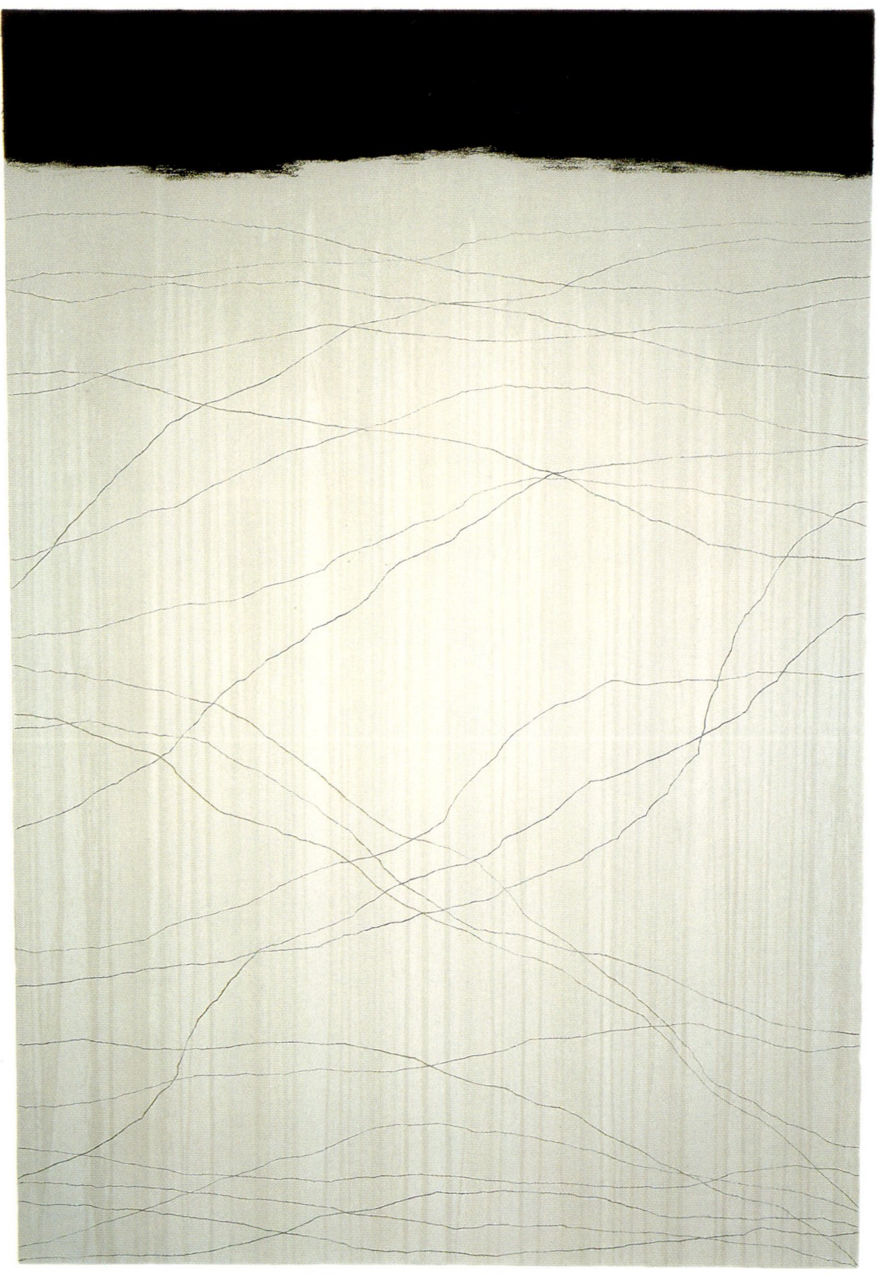

Bruce Robbins
American, b. 1948
Horizon
1996
90 in. x 60 in.

John Alexander
American, b. 1945
Bridal Path
1993
70 in. x 90 1/8 in.

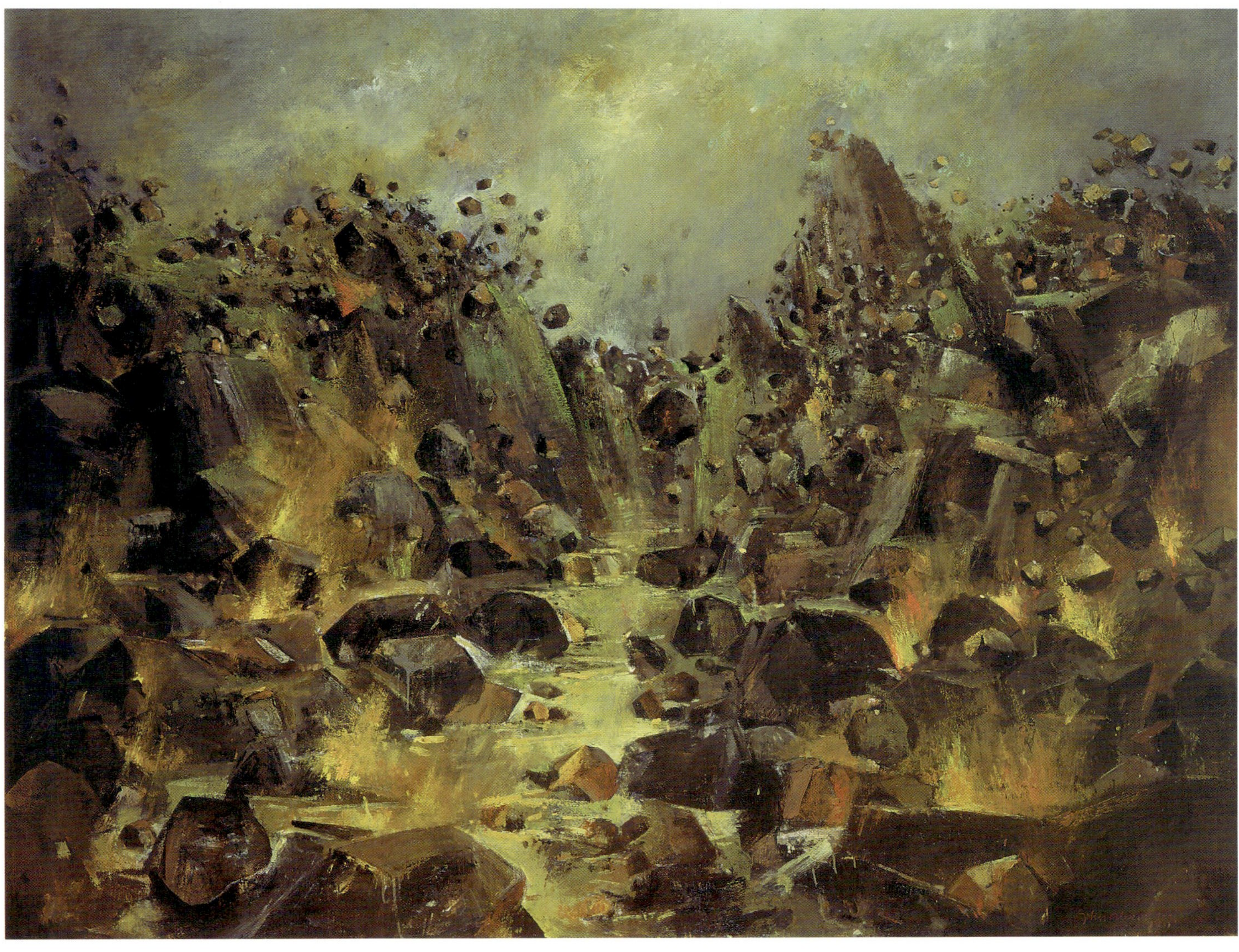

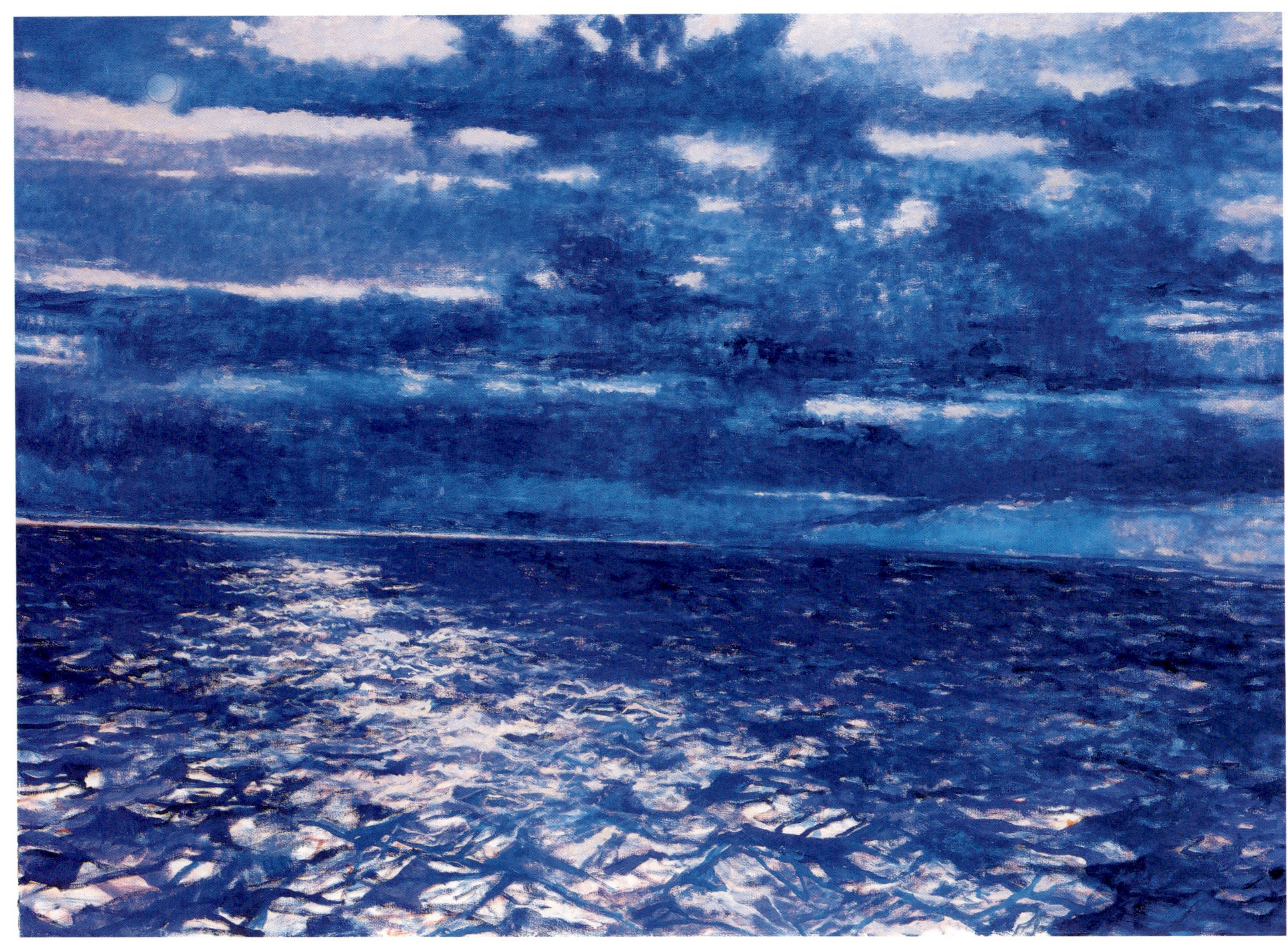

Peter Solow
American, b. 1952
Off Montauk
1996
60 in. x 80 in.

Alex Katz
American, b. 1927
Wildflowers III
1992
77 in. x 192 in.

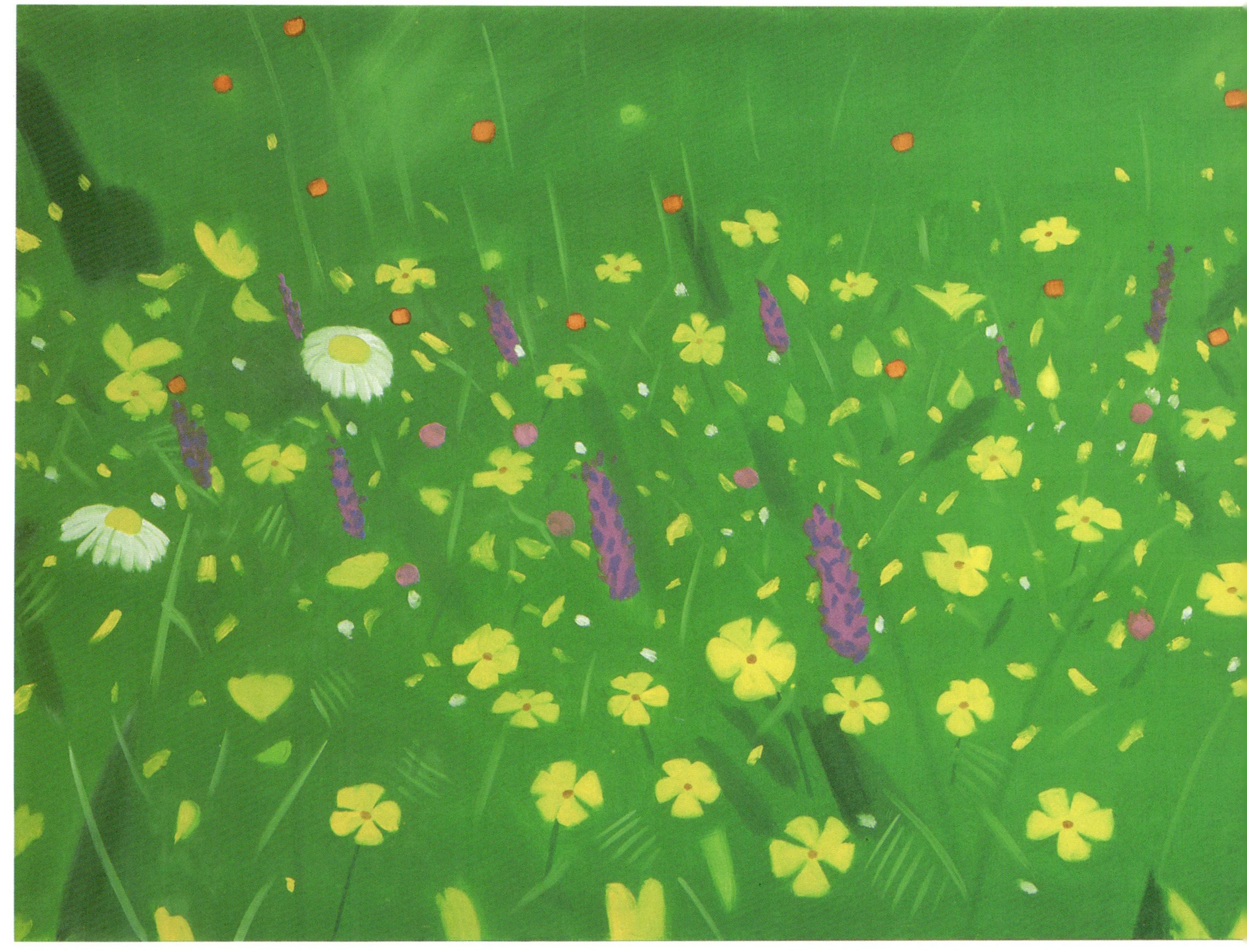

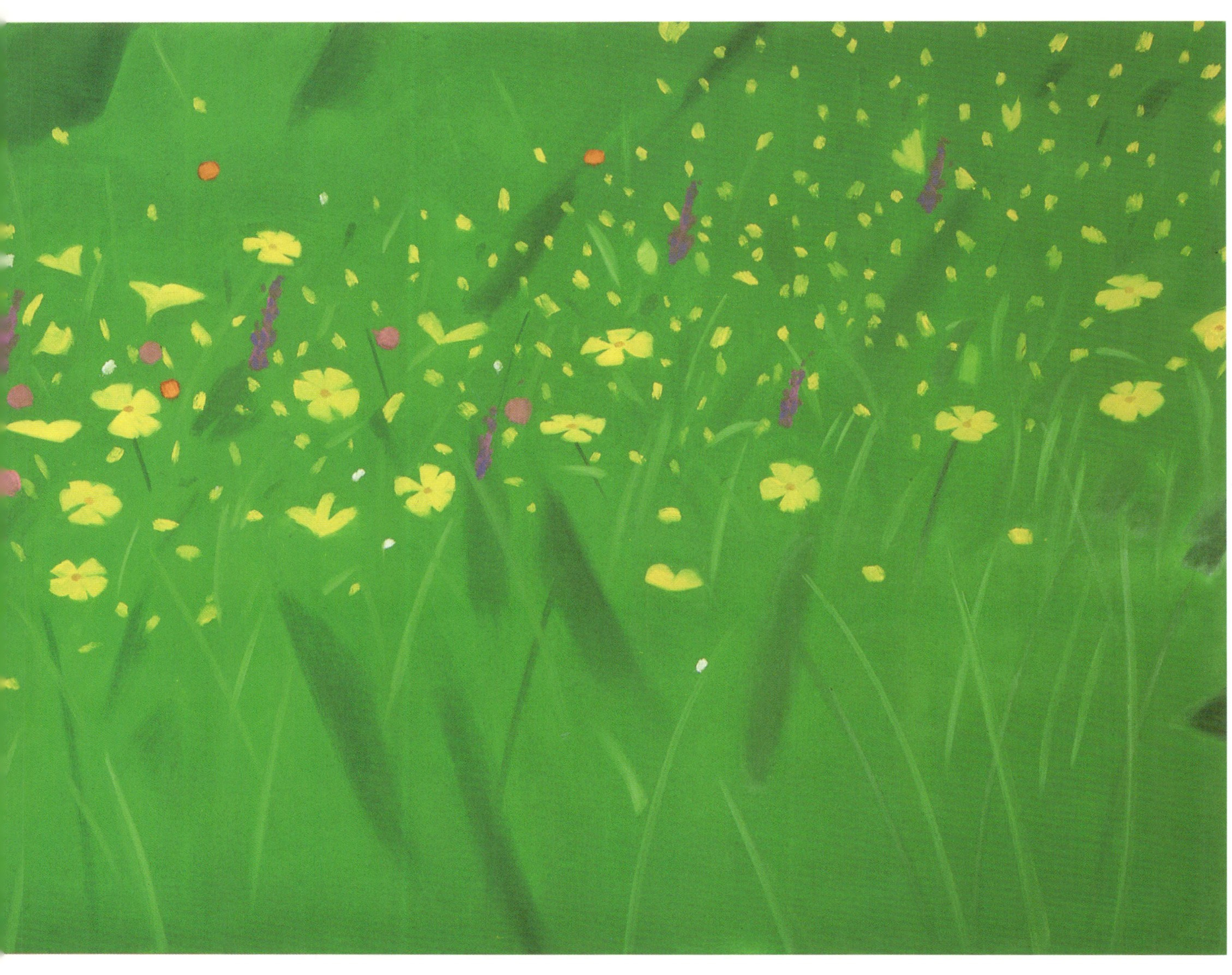

All dimensions are given in inches, height preceeding width.

John Alexander
American, b. 1945
Bridal Path
1993
oil on canvas
70 x 90 1/8
Lent by Marlborough Gallery, Inc., New York

Dozier Bell
American, b. 1957
Map #6
1995
oil and acrylic on linen
44 x 32
Lent by Schmidt-Bingham Gallery, New York

David Bierk
American, b. 1944
A Eulogy to Earth (History), Ancient River
1995
oil on steel
44 1/2 x 40 1/2
Lent by American Associated Artists,
New York

Jacqueline Bishop
American, b. 1955
System of Nature
1990
oil on masonite
18 7/8 x 47 5/8
Lent by Gerald Feffer and Monique Yingling

Alan Bray
American, b. 1946
Fresh Snow
1996
casein on panel
20 x 30
Lent by Schmidt-Bingham Gallery,
New York

Jerry Cutler
American, b. 1946
Monument
1993
oil on canvas
50 x 59
Lent by Center of the Earth Gallery,
Charlotte, North Carolina

Peter Edlund
American, b. 1959
Archives of the Earth
1996
oil on canvas
44 x 48
Lent by The Bailey Collection, Toronto
Courtesy of Jack Shainman Gallery,
New York

Robert Ferrandini
American, b. 1948
Gathering Samples Along Crystal Cove
1994
oil on panel
24 x 42
Lent by Gallery NAGA, Boston,
Massachusetts

April Gornik
American, b. 1953
Lightning at Twilight
1993
oil on linen
67 x 120
Lent by Edward Thorp Gallery, New York

Wade Hoefer
American, b. 1948
Agris II
1995
oil on linen mounted on wood
28 x 19 3/4
Lent from a private collection

Mark Innerst
American, b. 1952
Plume
1994
acrylic and aluminum leaf on board
with hand-built wooden frame
10 x 8
Lent by Curt Marcus Gallery, New York

Neil Jenney
American, b. 1945
Atmosphere
1985
oil on wood
36 x 69 1/2
Lent by Robert and Nancy Magoon

Jeff Joyce
American, b. 1956
Veil
1993
oil, alkyd, and graphite on canvas
72 x 60
Lent by the artist

Tobi Kahn
American, b. 1952
NAAHM-HWA
1994
acrylic on canvas over wood
40 x 50 x 2 1/2
Lent by the artist
Courtesy of Mary Ryan Gallery, New York

Alex Katz
American, b. 1927
Wildflowers III
1992
oil on canvas
77 x 192
Lent by Marlborough Gallery, Inc., New York

Holly Lane
American, b. 1954
Before Nightfall
1994
mixed media
29 x 24 x 5
Lent by Edith Dee Cofrin

Joan Nelson
American, b. 1958
Untitled (#396)
1994
acrylic, oil, powdered pigment, and
varnish on wood
10 x 10
Lent by Robert Miller Gallery, New York

Bruce Robbins
American, b. 1948
Horizon
1996
oil and encaustic on canvas
90 x 60
Lent by the artist

Alexis Rockman
American, b. 1962
Biosphere VI
1992
oil on wood
24 x 18
Lent from a private collection, New York

Peter Solow
American, b. 1952
Off Montauk
1996
oil on canvas
60 x 80
Lent by the artist

Pat Steir
American, b. 1940
November Night
1994-1995
oil on canvas
83 x 83
Lent by Robert Miller Gallery, New York

Adam Straus
American, b. 1956
McStop
1993
oil on canvas
84 x 60 x 2
Lent from a private collection, New York
Courtesy of Nohra Haime Gallery,
New York

Irene Valincius
American, born West Germany 1948
Fugitive Series: XIII
1994
oil and wax on canvas
36 x 30
Lent by Gallery NAGA, Boston,
Massachusetts

Hiram Williams
American, b. 1917
Mystical Events Over Bald Eagle
1992
oil on canvas
50 x 86
Lent by the artist